NILS SMITH & NICK RUNYON

CRYPTO FOR GOOD

Demystifying Cryptocurrencies for Nonprofits

Dunham
books

Published by Dunham Books

ISBN: 978-1-942464-65-5

CONTENTS

INTRODUCTION

Every other summer my wife's family gets together for a family reunion. This gathering usually takes place somewhere in the mountains. These mountain cabin reunions are a welcome reprieve from the summer heat and a chance to turn off our devices to share updates the old fashioned way: around the table, eating food.

This summer, one of my wife's uncles turned to me and said, "Do you know anything about Bitcoin?"

The conversation that followed among the relatives gathered was entertaining in its wild speculation—and also frightening in context. If I'm in a discussion about Bitcoin at a family reunion, this subject of cryptocurrency has hit the mainstream.

We have been working in nonprofit leadership, marketing, fundraising, and technology together for the past number of years. Over the past year, we have been fascinated with the blockchain, cryptocurrencies like Bitcoin, and the underlying technology these concepts are built upon. Our goal has always been to get ahead of the learning curve and work to educate nonprofit leaders on the opportunities that have the potential to drive their organizations forward.

What we find fascinating about this space is the speed at which technology is changing. More recently, we're seeing that blockchain technology has the possibility of replacing many of the industries and models that we rely on every day.

Serving as leaders of nonprofits ourselves, we believe that these changes will have significant implications for the next 10–20 years for nonprofit organizations.

As we've researched these issues, we keep hearing a familiar refrain:

"This feels like 1999."

When Netscape became a household term, and our horizons expanded across the World Wide Web, we never considered that one day we'd be wirelessly networking our houses to control power and water consumption through an app on our phones! However, with that experience behind us, we are learning what might be possible as ambiguous terms like Bitcoin and blockchain come into sharper focus.

So, what does cryptocurrency have to do with the nonprofit leader, and why should you care? The reality for all nonprofits is that donations drive their ability to accomplish their mission. Over the past decade, we have seen a continual shift in how donations are made, moving from checks in the mail to digital transactions on a website. Even as that shift continues, we are seeing a move from digital donations on a computer to digital donations on a mobile device. The world of fundraising is changing quickly around these new technologies, and it's our belief that cryptocurrency might just be the next shift that lies ahead.

We hope that leaders who read *Crypto for Good* will gain a basic understanding of this rapidly changing technology and begin to envision how blockchain technology and cryptocurrency might serve the mission of their organizations.

We invite you to join us on this journey to explore this new technological frontier!

~ Nick Runyon and Nils Smith

About the Authors

Nils Smith is the chief strategist of social media and innovation at Dunham+Company. With his extensive background in social media, innovation, and communication, Nils helps Dunham+Company's nonprofit clients create more impact through the strategic use of emerging technologies and advising on the latest social media and online best practices.

Before coming to Dunham+Company, Nils worked as the innovation pastor at Community Bible Church in San Antonio, Texas, one of the largest and fastest-growing churches in the country. While there, Nils led a talented team that developed their church's online engagement. He pioneered their use of mobile apps and TV apps and built the online church campus that now reaches 12,000 people in 400 cities each week.

He is the author of *The Social Media Guide for Ministry* and has since updated that book with the release of *The Social Media Guide.* His work has been featured in a wide range of publications and media outlets. Nils is a world-leading expert at the crossroads of social media and nonprofit strategy, and his expertise serves nonprofit clients every day.

Nils has a business management degree from Texas State University and holds a master's in ministry leadership from Rockbridge Seminary. He lives in New York City with his wife, Katie, and their two daughters.

Nick Runyon leads teams that are passionate about leveraging social media and technology to improve the lives of others. This mission is rooted in a career that spans Silicon Valley startup and global nonprofit ministry experience.

As the executive director of a nonprofit, Nick's team builds marketing and technology solutions for churches and ministries around the world.

Early in his career, as marketing director at PFL.com, Nick advanced a performance-based advertising strategy that helped PFL become a four-time INC 500 winner as one of the fastest- growing companies in America.

In 2008, Nick moved from business to ministry, applying performance metrics and analysis to digital evangelism with Silicon Valley based Global Media Outreach. Serving as chief operating officer, Nick developed a global marketing strategy and technology that helped GMO reach over 1.2 billion people with the biblical message of Jesus Christ during his time with the organization.

Believing that making others better makes us all better, Nick participates in coaching, training, and speaking engagements to share his experience and improve the organizations and businesses of others. Nick has helped train over 60 Christian organizations in strengthening evangelism efforts through the use of technology and is a sought-after speaker on the subject of digital marketing, ministry, and nonprofit leadership.

Together, Nils and Nick co-host the *Social Media Church Podcast*. Through that podcast, they help other people improve their ability to do good and are engaged in work that places their expertise in service of the nonprofit clients they serve.

Who Should Read 'Crypto for Good'?

We hope that through this book we can share a little of what we've learned and help you and your organization think about how your nonprofit organization might benefit from this new technology in the future.

If this is as big a shift in technology as the mainstream adoption of the internet in the late 90s, those of us who lead teams and organizations should be working to understand what opportunities might exist and how our teams can be positioned to capitalize on those opportunities in the years to come.

CHAPTER 1

A Brief History of Money and the U.S. Dollar

To understand cryptocurrencies we must consider currency itself. Have you ever stopped to think about what money or currency is?

Currency refers explicitly to money used as a medium of exchange. At the core of this exchange is value. Currency is created to represent value. When an exchange of goods or services occurs, there is an agreed upon value associated with the currency used for the transaction.

Currencies like the U.S. dollar are fiat currency. *Fiat* simply means that some authority has determined the value of the currency. These monies have no intrinsic value. The backing government maintains its value. This means that you cannot trade in your money to the government in exchange for gold or something else of value. It is simply used as a representation of value which is defined by exchange rates.

Historically, currency is established by a nation. The U.S. dollar is represented in the form of a paper bill and designated as legal tender by the government. Foreign exchange markets determine the relative values of different currencies recognized by each nation. These markets are defined in many ways by the number of transactions, and various factors affect the agreed upon value of each currency, which is constantly in flux relative to one another.

Early Value Exchange

The exchange of value has been core to every society since the beginning of man. Early in history, this exchange was conducted through bartering goods and services, often including cattle or vegetables. These items of value began to shift to currency, first in China, somewhere around 1100 B.C. People would use small replicas of goods cast in gold. This practice spread and progressed to the first official currency minted in 600 B.C. in Lydia (now a part of Turkey). The first currency was a physical coin featuring a roaring lion.

It's fascinating to think about the core need for value exchange that has always existed and the challenges that are present in the bartering of goods and services. The existence of currency itself brings value to society by simplifying the process.

Currencies steadily progressed over the next few centuries as paper money was introduced in 1290 A.D. But the transition to paper money did not catch on until

1661 A.D. This innovation allowed for currency to be mass produced without the reliance on raw metals like gold and silver. As populations grew, the systems of value exchange needed to mature and progress.

Money and Innovation

Technology innovation around currency began to accelerate in the 1800s when Western Union pioneered what we would now see as "e-money" with electronic transfers taking place through the telegraph. More than 100 years ago, our society recognized a need for electronic money transfers!

In the 1920s, department stores and oil companies began to extend credit to customers, and in the 1950s, credit cards began to enter the scene. One of the most popular credit cards was the Diners Club that charged merchants a 7% fee on each transaction. In the 1960s, credit cards began to see mass adoption with companies like Bank of America and American Express entering the scene.

Similar to most new innovations, regulation came very late. The first level of regulation arrived in 1968 with the Truth in Lending Act, which standardized methods of calculating annual percentage rates. As regulation around credit cards continued to mature and evolve in the following three decades, so did the adoption of credit cards and continued expansion in the field.

Digital innovation around financial transactions

picked up steam in 1999 when European banks began offering mobile banking. More advancement brought contactless payments cards in 2008, first issued in the United Kingdom. Naturally, credit cards/debit cards have become the norm for most transactions worldwide, and now digital payment systems like Apple Pay in retail locations or peer-to-peer transactions using Venmo are commonplace.

In 2018, the exchange of value has primarily moved to digital means. Globalization of the economy has shifted the way many transactions today are made, opening up new opportunities for higher efficiency as well as the need for greater transparency and accountability in currency exchange.

With these changes come many questions about security and privacy. Terms like *decentralization* sound subversive in a world where currency has been established and governed by an institutional system backed primarily by government structures. The world is changing, and it can feel quite confusing.

The Stability of the U.S. Dollar

The U.S. dollar provides stability to the world's financial markets. To understand the implications of cryptocurrencies, we should also review this currency and the dollar's role in history.

The dollar has been stable our entire lives. Most

people have never really questioned where it came from, what it's worth, and how it works.

The U.S. dollar was created in 1778 and fully established in 1792 under the leadership of Alexander Hamilton. Actual gold backed the early dollar, as well as silver in later years. In the 1930s, during the Great Depression, the U.S. dollar experienced its most significant change when the gold standard was abandoned. Every other global currency at the time had the same experience. Many factors led to this and with the benefit of time, we now see this change was inevitable.

This shift created our first questions about trust, and many people began hoarding gold coins and other stores of value. Even today, nearly 100 years later, gold is seen as a haven for investors in times of financial disruption and market downturns.

Historically, the U.S. dollar has had one of the most consistent values making it an ideal candidate as an international reserve currency. Other countries hold large amounts of U.S. dollars as part of their foreign exchange reserves. According to the Federal Reserve Bank of New York in 2013, there was an estimated $1.2 trillion worth of U.S. dollars in circulation (https://www.newyorkfed.org/aboutthefed/fedpoint/fed01.html).

Every form of currency has a story. Every currency has gone through changes, and exchanges of money will continue to change. There is no doubt that the U.S. dollar will also continue to evolve as well.

Today, the emerging innovation that could radically transform how value is exchanged is the creation and proliferation of cryptocurrencies. It seems that this may be another evolution of money. Alternatively, the experiment may fizzle out under the pressure of complex global systems and the governments that rely on the current financial realities of today. Time will tell. However, we believe cryptocurrencies could be here to stay, so it's imperative to understand how they work and the implications for funding charitable causes.

Summary

Currency is a medium of agreed upon value used for exchange.

1. Currencies have always changed throughout time in medium and ways that transactions are made using them.
2. Digital exchange is nothing new in terms of currency transactions.
3. The U.S. dollar has gone through many changes itself including no longer being backed by gold.
4. The value of the U.S. dollar is very stable in comparison to most other global currencies.

CHAPTER 2

An Introduction to Blockchain

While watching baseball on TV recently, a commercial for one of the big computer companies came on between innings. It was one of the worst commercials ever, as if repeatnig all the buzzwords of the day would convince consumers that they're smart. But the commercial actually revealed the company didn't really know what they're talking about. Among this wall of words without context was talk about *AI, Blockchain, Cloud,* and *app integration.*

The whole world is like this right now. If a company just mentions blockchain as part of their quarterly plans on a shareholder call, their stock price jumps. Everyone is talking about Bitcoin and blockchain, but most of us feel completely lost. A lot of people are talking about this stuff. About half know something about it. Very few have a good grasp on the topic.

For those new to the conversation, and looking for a little guidance, we intend to simplify and educate. To start, let's talk about the technology behind this entire conversation: Blockchain.

What Is Blockchain?

Blockchain is basically a database. This is the easiest way to think about it.

A database, in the simplest terms, records and stores information. One can also think about a database as a ledger. Like an accounting ledger, blockchain is used to record transactions or changes to the ledger as new entries are made.

The unique thing about the blockchain database is that it is distributed. It doesn't exist on any one computer, but on many.

When our elementary school class used to visit the library, we learned how to look up books using the library's database. The central server that housed all the data was called the *Master*. Various terminals located around the library were *Slave* computers that could only access the *Master*.

In very simple terms, the internet works this way. Your personal browser is used to access a server, retrieve files, images, and data from various servers to then display a website. If I want to update my website for the world, I only need to login and update my files hosted on the server.

Blockchain technology is different. Rather than a Master/Slave relationship, the database is Master/Master, or rather peer-to-peer. Blockchain uses multiple computers connected in a peer-to-peer network with each computer hosting the entire database. This description is overly simplistic, but the main idea is that the blockchain is completely distributed. It does not exist in one place, but many places, and all versions are exactly the same.

How can this be? How can a distributed database be kept in sync and up to date? We'll cover that in a bit. First, let's talk a bit more about the implications of a distributed database.

Because the blockchain doesn't exist in a central location, authority for the database is decentralized. No central authority or governing body controls the blockchain, and this is something that is fundamental to our understanding of blockchain, cryptocurrencies, smart contracts, and all the other concepts that use the blockchain to exist.

This technology is both distributed (lives on multiple computers) and decentralized (not controlled).

The blockchain represents the most innovative and significant advance in computer science since the invention and proliferation of the internet. Like the internet, it can be used in all sectors of all economy and all industries. Blockchain technology has already been adopted and used by various organizations and companies that want to provide efficient and fast service to their thousands of clients and customers worldwide.

If blockchain is a database that is both decentralized

and distributed, then we have something that is very unique. Anyone, anywhere is able to view the database at any time. Anyone is also allowed to add to the database at any time. No permissions are needed.

But, for this kind of freedom of use, some rules must exist. What's more, they must be followed and enforced.

This is where the blockchain is, in our opinion, amazing.

How Does Blockchain Technology Work?

Each new entry to the database is a block. When these blocks are stacked, or "chained" together, we get the blockchain.

We're getting deep into this now... but hang on, we're almost there!)

For the blockchain technology to be used as a distributed ledger, it must be managed by a P2P (peer-to-peer) network that adheres to a specific protocol for validation of new blocks and inter-node communications as well. All data recorded on the blockchain cannot be altered without having to alter all subsequent blocks.

Ensuring that all subsequent blocks match every time a new transaction is added to the chain is vital. This is accomplished through some complex cryptographic computing using hash functions. We know this is very technical, but it's vital to understand because this is what makes cryptocurrencies so powerful.

The Bitcoin Wiki[1] describes the process in this way.

> Each block contains, among other things, a record of some or all recent transactions, and a reference to the block that came immediately before it. It also contains an answer to a difficult-to-solve mathematical puzzle - the answer to which is unique to each block. New blocks cannot be submitted to the network without the correct answer - the process of "mining" is essentially the process of competing to be the next to find the answer that "solves" the current block. The mathematical problem in each block is extremely difficult to solve, but once a valid solution is found, it is very easy for the rest of the network to confirm that the solution is correct. There are multiple valid solutions for any given block - only one of the solutions needs to be found for the block to be solved.

A Secure System

Locks keep honest people honest. The thieves are going to find a way around the locks sooner or later. But many believe that blockchain technology solves the problem of

1 https://en.bitcoin.it/wiki/Block

security through transparency. If everything is visible and verifiable, the database cannot be hacked.

The issue of online security is very real. More than 171 million records were exposed in 2017 through more than 1,100 data breaches. What is really scary is that this is a 475% increase from 2016! We are constantly receiving notifications about our financial, medical, and business data that has been compromised.

Thieves aren't likely to change their behavior any time soon. And, the world is only becoming more networked and more dependent upon digital technology. The question then becomes, how can true security exist in a world where trust in systems and people is increasingly called into question?

Many believe that for true security to exist, a system needs to:

1. Store Records
2. Enable Anyone to Verfity Facts

No one can cheat the system by editing records because everyone would be watching and keeping track of records as they are created and edited. Verification can happen at any time.

Some questions exist about the cryptography and hash functions used to verify the blockchain. As far as we know, the current hash functions are not able to be manipulated or predicted. We believe that the outputs are always unique and will always be unique, so for now, the blockchai n is un-hackable. We'll discuss more about security when we discuss digital wallets, public and private keys, and individual security.

Summary

1. The blockchain is a database.
2. The blockchain is both distributed and decentralized.
3. Blocks are added to the chain using complex cryptographic hash functions, which are simultaneously verifying the authenticity of the entire chain.
4. The open visibility of the blockchain and its distributed nature make it unlikely to be manipulated.

CHAPTER 3

Cryptocurrencies and Bitcoin

With the concept of currency and the technology of the blockchain under our belts, let's combine these two things and dive into the core focus of this book: cryptocurrency. Now it gets fun!

Cryptocurrency Defined

> ***Cryptocurrency:*** *A digital currency that uses encryption (cryptography) to generate money and to verify transactions. Transactions are added to a public ledger – also called a Transaction BlockChain – and new coins are created through a process known as mining.*[2]

There's a lot to unpack in this definition. The first term in this definition is *digital currency*. Understanding the concept of digital currency is the most accessible aspect of cryptocurrency to follow because so much of our lives have already gone digital. Most of our transactions are

2 https://cryptocurrencyfacts.com/

already digital with e-commerce, online bill pay, and other electronic exchanges of money. It seems only natural that our currency would also be digital.

Digital things are convenient, but rarely do we equate *digital* with *safe*. Hackers, security, and identity theft have given rise to a $153 billion cyber security market. (https://www.statista.com/statistics/595182/worldwide-security-as-a-service-market-size/) How then, can we have a digital currency that is stable and secure?

Historically we have relied on third-party financial institutions to provide the verification for transactions and ensure security. But through the blockchain as described in the last chapter, these transactions now become much more efficient and secure.

Transaction details and the creation of cryptocurrency are not stored or processed in one location but instead through the peer-to-peer network on the blockchain. This shared network creates both transparency and security for all transactions. Security exists in this system because there are no central authorities tracking transactions. Instead, every transaction is visible to everyone, and the ledger is stored publicly across a global network rather than on central servers owned by a single party, government, or organization. This aspect of cryptocurrency is extremely significant.

Historically, much of our financial system has been discrete. A central authority is responsible for the financial security of fiat currencies. However, the blockchain allows for all transactions to be public while also maintaining necessary privacy within the transactions.

Anyone can see Bitcoin trades occur and for how much. However, the identity of the two parties involved in a deal displays in the form of *public keys*, a proxy identifier unique to every individual. This feature of the blockchain creates a significant level of privacy in all transactions with minimal data shared publicly.

Mining

The definition above references *mining*. Let's unpack this idea a bit.

In cryptocurrency networks, mining is a validation of transactions. For this effort, successful miners obtain new cryptocurrency as a reward. The reward decreases transaction fees by creating a complementary incentive to contribute to the processing power of the network.[3]

At the core of this digital currency is encryption, and mining is a complicated process of verifying all transactions using cryptography. This entire process is known as *hashing*. Blocks in the chain are hashed together, verifying authenticity, and miners or people solving the math problems that verify transactions are rewarded with coins.

This verification process changes everything about the way we transfer value, which is the core purpose of

---

3 https://en.wikipedia.org/wiki/Cryptocurrency#Mining

cryptocurrency itself.

Mining is the core function that creates the incentive for miners to contribute their computing power to the network, thereby creating greater efficiency and stability for all transactions processed through the blockchain.

Miners are those in the network competing to collect transaction data, verify transactions against the existing blockchain (existing ledger), and solve a cryptographic puzzle that allows them to add a block of recent transactions to the blockchain (receiving new coins as a reward). (source: https://cryptocurrencyfacts.com/what-is-a-blockchain/)

Getting to Know Bitcoin

Let's take a look at the most popular form of cryptocurrency to understand how this all fits together: Bitcoin. In the next chapter, we will discuss the thousands of new currencies that exist, but foundational for so much of this development of cryptocurrency has been the creation, maturity, and mass appeal of Bitcoin.

Bitcoin was created by an unknown person or group of people that developed the digital currency under the name Satoshi Nakamoto. In 2008 Satoshi released a white paper that you can still read on bitcoin.org.

In January 2009, the first coin was released as the Genesis coin. The first coin was awarded to a "cypherpunk" named Hal Finney who downloaded the Bitcoin software on its release date and received 10 coins from Satoshi. Satoshi mined an estimated 1 million bitcoins before disappearing in 2010.

In the first few years, the value of Bitcoin fluctuated tremendously. In 2012 alone, the price started as low as $0.30 and spiked to as high as $31.50 before dipping again to under $5 later in the year. In September of that same year, The Bitcoin Foundation was founded to "accelerate the standardization, protection, and promotion of the open source protocol" which brought a level of stability to the platform. From 2013 to 2016, the price of Bitcoin grew tremendously, starting at $13.30 and rising to $998 on January 1, 2017. Volatility struck again in 2017, as the price soared as high as $19,666 before dipping as low as $5,848 in 2018. At the time of this publication (August 2018), a single Bitcoin is worth $7,802.

Despite the volatility, it's overwhelming to think that something could have a value of $0.30 in 2012 and just five years later be trading for an amount of $19,666! It's also not hard to then understand why this cryptocurrency has received so much attention.

Let's get into the coin itself. The unit of account of the Bitcoin system is called a *Bitcoin*. Bitcoin launched with the idea of creating artificial scarcity, and a maximum number of Bitcoins was established at 21 million. As Bitcoin distributions become smaller and smaller over time (to maintain scarcity), experts estimate that the mining of the last coin will occur sometime in 2140.

It is also possible to divide Bitcoin into smaller amounts, similar to how a dollar is divisible by pennies or even fractions of a cent. Owning less than one coin is possible. Bitcoins can be fractioned off down to one-millionth of a Bitcoin. When all coins are released, miners will then be awarded not through the distribution of Bitcoins, but by transaction fees.

To make a transaction on the Bitcoin blockchain, you must create a valid private key which establishes a Bitcoin address, and within seconds you can make a trade. This private key is at the core where the store of value lies. If lost, so are the Bitcoins in the account. Some estimate that 20% of all existing Bitcoins are unable to be recovered. Lost coins only add to the scarcity of the currency itself.

Maintaining the security of one's private key is critical to keeping one's account safe. The individual is solely responsible for their private key. This individual responsibility is one of the most exciting and essential concepts to understand when using cryptocurrency. What this means is that the security of your currency is now fully on the individual rather than the institution (the bank). One's private key opens everything; without it, one's Bitcoins are inaccessible. With it, a thief can take everything in the account.

Cryptocurrency Wallets

The tool used in transacting Bitcoin and other

cryptocurrencies is a *cryptocurrency wallet*. Historically we have known wallets to store money, but a cryptocurrency wallet functions more like a credit card than a wallet as we know it. While a cryptocurrency wallet doesn't store your actual cryptocurrencies, it is used to store your private keys or digital credentials needed to access to the cryptocurrencies and to transact them.

Cryptocurrency wallets are essentially a software program that stores your private and public keys to interact with the blockchain. When someone sends you money on the blockchain, they are signing off ownership of their coins to your digital wallet address. When you go to use these coins, your private key stored in your wallet must match the public address assigned to the currency. At this point, ownership of these coins has shifted and the balance in your digital wallet increases and the senders will decrease. While there is no actual exchange of coins, the transaction is stored on the blockchain, and the ownership of the value is visible in your digital wallet.

Here are many types of cryptocurrency wallets that people use to store these keys and to make transactions on the blockchain:

- **Online:** runs on the cloud and accessible through any desktop or mobile computing device
- **Mobile:** runs on a mobile app on your phone
- **Hardware:** stored on physical devices like a USB drive

- **Paper Wallet:** accessed through a QR code printed on a piece of paper and must be transferred to a software wallet to be transacted

We hope that you now have a basic understanding of cryptocurrency and the popular Bitcoin cryptocurrency. Bitcoin is only one of thousands of cryptocurrencies in existence, with many others expanding on the underlying technology to deliver value beyond the currency itself.

Summary

1. Cryptocurrencies are a digital currency that uses cryptography to generate money and verify transactions.
2. Blockchain is the technology that powers cryptocurrency creating greater efficiency and security.
3. Bitcoin was the first cryptocurrency to have mass appeal.
4. While Bitcoin's value has grown tremendously, it has also remained volatile.
5. Cryptocurrency wallets do not transact currencies or even store them, but rather store your private keys or digital credentials.

CHAPTER 4

2,000 Cryptocurrencies and Counting

As Nick helped his new bride into the cab of his Chevy truck, taking extra care to get the train of her wedding dress safely inside, he closed the door only to see "I found my wife on eBay" written in shoe polish on the passenger door window. His college buddies standing around watching them leave the reception thought this was hilarious.

eBay launched in the fall of 1995, and Nick fell in love with the idea. By 1998, he was buying and selling from his college dorm room. Over the next few years, he would buy snow skis, bindings, poles, and ski boots, individually at a low cost, and outfit himself and his friends for a spring break ski trip. After the trip, he would list the items as a complete package deal, add a little creative writing and some good photos, and sell the complete package for a profit.

He bought and sold motorcycles, cars, fishing gear—whatever he wanted on eBay. He would use these items and then resell them, usually making a profit. And he never did worse than breaking even.

eBay was amazing back then. The auction environment was an exciting way to buy things. It took timing and market research to buy at a good price and make money on the sales.

eBay provided easy access to scarce items for consumers willing to navigate the auction environment. This is why it was brilliant. I could find access to purchase things that were hard to find (new or used items in good condition) and sell my used items to the market created by eBay's online platform.

But, eBay wasn't very easy to use early on. Unscrupulous sellers would list a popular item for sale, collect payment for the item, and never ship the product. Buyers had to send checks in the mail to make payments. User ratings were some help, but buyers and sellers resorted to developing their own systems of vetting to make sure they didn't get scammed. On larger dollar transactions, like vehicles, buyers and sellers would often meet for a transfer and renegotiate the deal on site. The terms of the digital auction had very little authority in the real world.

Even with all of these problems, eBay was a game changer. Broad access to scarce items offered on a platform that enabled buyers and sellers to make a transaction.

Buying and selling cryptocurrency is kind of like the eBay experience in the early days. The process seems simple enough, but questions remain. There are risks.

Making a cryptocurrency transaction is still kind of a murky process, and users must understand the risks to keep themselves safe.

There are a lot of different ways to buy, sell, and manage your cryptocurrencies. We're going to help you get started.

Brokers and Exchanges

If you've read anything about cryptocurrencies or Bitcoin in the past year, you've probably heard of the San Francisco–based digital currency exchange Coinbase. Coinbase is important because it is one of the first companies to help bring cryptocurrency transactions into the mainstream. In the following pages, we want to help readers understand the different kinds of exchanges and their implications for financial transactions.

Cryptocurrency exchanges operate like a stock broker for making stock purchases. Customers can exchange fiat currencies for a few of the most popular cryptocurrencies including Bitcoin, Ethereum, and Litecoin. Other exchanges allow users to swap one cryptocurrency for another without any fiat exchange involved.

Digital currency exchanges (DCE) like Coinbase are the easiest way to buy and sell cryptocurrencies. At the time of this publication, we see dozens of crypto exchanges in operation with varying levels of features and requirements.

Fiat Exchanges

The first type of exchange that we'll discuss are those that allow users to exchange U.S. dollars, euros, or other government-backed currencies for cryptocurrency. Coinbase, Gemini, and Kraken are among the most popular DCEs that offer fiat exchanges.

After creating an account with an exchange's online platform, users go through an account verification process to verify their credit card, debit card, or bank account details for ACH transfers. Purchasing is usually a simple process of selecting the cryptocurrency you'd like to purchase, entering your amount, and making the transaction.

Most fiat exchanges are widely available, though there are limitations by country or state depending on which exchange you're using. Also, we've found that most fiat exchanges only deal in the more establish cryptocurrencies like Bitcoin and Ethereum.

The massive fluctuations in the cryptocurrency market has opened the door for traders attempting to capitalize on investments through cryptocurrency trading: "Cryptocurrency, also known as digital assets, trading is the buying, selling or holding of cryptocurrencies such a Bitcoin (XBT), Ethereum (ETH), Litecoin (LTC) amongst others, with the aim of generating a profit from short, medium or long term fluctuations in their prices."[4]

---

4 https://support.kraken.com/hc/en-us/articles/360000674406-Introduction-to-cryptocurrency-trading

Cryptocurrency to Cryptocurrency Exchanges

The second type of exchanges we will review are DCEs that give users access to cryptocurrencies through the exchange of other cryptos only. No U.S. dollars or euros being exchanged here!

Users need to first exchange fiat currency for cryptocurrency on a Fiat Exchange, like Coinbase, and then make a transfer into a digital wallet or account in a cryptocurrency exchange in order to buy or sell through these exchanges.

Unlike Fiat Exchanges, Cryptocurrency Exchanges open users to the larger landscape of digital coins. Log in to a popular exchange like Binance[5], and you'll see dozens of cryptos listed with names like Ripple, Aeron, TRON, ETHOS, and Verge.

Beyond Bitcoin and Ethereum, two of the earliest and most popular cryptocurrencies, there are thousands of other coins available for trade. Sites like Binance give exchange rates for these coins in Bitcoin (BTC).

So Many Coins!

By now you hopefully have some understanding of the cryptocurrency landscape, the underlying blockchain technology, and how these cryptocurrencies compare to fiat currency like the U.S. dollar. "But why," you might

---

5 https://www.binance.com

ask, "are there so many kinds of digital coins?"

Blockchain technology and the Bitcoin protocol opened up the door for digital currency. Since then, many new coins have been created for different purposes. Some coins represent different technology protocols, while other coins exist simply because of a difference in purpose. In every case, the blockchain's core concepts of decentralized ledgers and public verification of digital activity are opening the door to all kinds of creative uses for this technology.

Each concept is matched with a digital coin as a store of value which can be traded and exchanged.

No two coins are alike. Bitcoin is built on the idea of digital scarcity. The distribution of Bitcoin is modeled after the scarcity of gold. Miners, as we discussed in earlier chapters, are rewarded with Bitcoin when they complete cryptographic calculations and add blocks to the blockchain. These calculations become increasingly difficult over time and the total number of Bitcoins is capped at 21 million. By comparison, the second most popular cryptocurrency, Ethereum, has no cap and has completely different underlying technology.

Ethereum was created as a blockchain platform to carry smart contracts. Smart contracts keep track of exchanges of money, property, shares, or other valuable assets. We've already discussed how the blockchain is like an accounting ledger. Instead of only tracking transactions of funds, the Ethereum blockchain uses smart contracts to execute on conditions or contingencies within the agreed exchange. If we issue an Ethereum–supported smart contract to you for the purchase of your home, the smart contract can act like an escrow service and verify that funds are present on the blockchain before releasing digital assets like the deed and title of your home to me. Ethereum coins are distributed to those who add these smart contract blocks to the Ethereum blockchain.

These two simple examples, Bitcoin and Ethereum, show the difference between cryptocurrency coins and their purpose and technology. As developers come up with new concepts that can be supported by blockchain technology, we are sure to see new coins emerge into the cryptocurrency market. At the time of this publication, there are well over 1,500 different cryptos.

For example, Ripple is a digital currency designed for the banking world. Instead of exchanging fiat currency across international borders, Ripple provides a way to transfer fiat currency into digital currency and back again with much lower exchange rates.

Another example is TRON, which is a digital coin that leverages blockchain's ability to track digital ownership and facilitate a decentralized entertainment content sharing platform. According to their white paper, TRON's open, decentralized platform will allow creators of digital content (music, movies, art, etc.) to cut out middlemen such as the Apple Store and Google Play

Store. Content producers will thus be able to obtain funds directly from consumers.

The list goes on and on with new ideas being developed every day.

Summary

1. Cryptocurrency can be received into a digital wallet or purchased through a Fiat exchange like Coinbase using U.S. dollars.
2. Thousands of cryptocurrencies exist, each with their own store of value.
3. Cryptocurrencies are exchanged through Digital Currency Exchanges or DCEs.
4. Understanding the purpose and use of a digital coin is essential before making any kind of investment.

CHAPTER 5

Advantages of Cryptocurrency

Cryptocurrency as a mainstream store of value has the potential to change the way the world trades and manages assets. As the underlying blockchain technology develops and becomes more widely used, we anticipate the benefits of cryptocurrency to only increase. These possibilities became clear to Nick during a recent experience on his block.

Every Thursday morning, the streets in his neighborhood are lined with trash cans. On this particular week, his oldest son was on trash duty for their house. As they were eating breakfast on trash collection morning, the sound of a garbage truck could be heard rumbling through their neighborhood. Suddenly his son bolted from the breakfast table, nearly spilling his bowl of Rice Krispies, to make a mad dash for the garage and get their garbage can out to the street before the garbage truck passed by. Nobody wants a week's worth of trash sitting in the garage for another seven days!

Usually, getting the garbage out to the curb passes

without incident. But this week, a woman stopped by their house on Thursday afternoon. With a check in hand, she told Nick's wife, "I found this out on the street and thought you might want it back."

It was a check that they had deposited through the banking app on Nick's phone and then thrown away. The check had been tossed in the trash, never to be seen again... or so they thought. Clearly, this check had somehow escaped the trash bag, the garbage can, and the garbage truck to find itself carried by the wind throughout their neighborhood.

Have you ever thought about how much personal data is visible to anyone who sees a check that you write? How many eyeballs land on each check written from your account?

Someone who receives a check from you knows your name, your address, your bank, the checking account number, and the bank routing number. They know who you paid, the amount paid, and the purpose for the payment (if written on the memo line).

It's kind of crazy when you think about it. But, this is the system that we know, trust, and has served us well. And in 2018, the information available through the internet allows anyone to cross reference the data from your handwritten check with other publicly available data, creating a serious security risk.

Digital transactions via credit and debit cards improved data privacy to a point, but these cards have also opened up new opportunities for data to be stolen and misused that did not previously exist. In this chapter, we will dig into some of the immediate advantages of cryptocurrency when it comes to security.

Security and Identity Theft

As you have read in the previous chapters, crypto offers security that exists due to blockchain technology. Every week we hear of major databases that have been hacked resulting in financial information being stolen. And there are even more databases being hacked accessing personal financial data that you are likely not hearing about.

The blockchain presents immediate solutions to many of the vulnerabilities existing within digital financial transactions. Blockchain exchanges are giving increased security through all cryptocurrency transactions utilizing the foundational security measure of cryptography that we previously mentioned.

The individual is now in control of the security of their funds rather than relying on an institution for protection. This is critical to understand, as most people have come to trust banks and other financial institutions to secure their money (as the days of hiding all of your cash money in your mattress are well behind us). While you cannot store or secure your cryptocurrency in your mattress, you are in control of how you secure it, whether you do that through cold storage, a specific digital wallet, or other measures.

Further connected to the security of cryptocurrency transactions is the security of your identity. In digital transactions with fiat currency, the processor of your transaction has access to your full credit line along with a significant amount of personal information, including your name and address. In contrast, cryptocurrency transactions can be conducted anonymously with only a user's public key being visible on the blockchain. As long as you protect your private key and connected identity, the public key is safe and disconnected from your personal details.

When it comes to cryptocurrency transactions, you only send the necessary information to complete the transaction, which eliminates the need for unnecessary sharing of personal identity information. While the anonymity of cryptocurrency has been one of the significant issues that many have with crypto—which has led to much of the illegal activity connected to it—the personal security aspect can be valuable to all. It is our belief that as regulations continue to mature, the anonymity enabling illegal activity will be minimized and the personal security will be maximized to a greater extent.

Speed

Have you ever bought or sold a house? While much of the paperwork might have gone digital, it still feels like the process hasn't changed in decades. There are so many layers to verification with the title company, banks, and other third parties. Have ever asked if there might be a better way considering all the new technology that exists? Well, much of the blockchain technology will bring resolution to the speed of these transactions creating fast, secure, and clearly defined transfers of value.

Whether a transaction is large or small with cryptocurrency, it is essentially instantaneous. Some cryptocurrencies like Bitcoin take a matter of minutes to complete a transaction while others like Ripple require only a few seconds.

Fiat transactions involving a third party, by comparison, often involve a holding period while details are confirmed. It is essential for security with separate centralized database systems. This process can take days to complete depending on the size of the transaction and what specifically is being exchanged. It is especially true in international transactions where speed can be a significant issue.

Cryptocurrencies promise faster transactions because they don't require processing through various financial institutions. Of course, this lack of regulation is also a major blocker for the wider adoption of cryptocurrencies, as banks and governments rush to understand the onward implications of cross-border transactions through crypto.

Universal Access

Universal access to cryptocurrencies is a unique benefit that opens doors for advancement globally. For individuals in countries where the currency is unstable, saving money did not make sense and exchanging to other currencies was inefficient or even inaccessible.

Today, anyone with internet access can send and receive cryptocurrencies freely. Crypto transactions are not bound by exchange rates and have the potential to create greater efficiencies for global trade. This provides incredible value to those in countries without a stable currency as well as a natural value for more international transactions to take place.

Not only does cryptocurrency add value to transactions globally, it also creates greater efficiencies for global organizations to transfer funds or stores of values to different entities across the globe without significant transfer fees. For decades, these transactions have primarily been funneled through Western Union, often with great challenges in developing countries. The developing efficiencies of cryptocurrency immediately resolve so many of these challenges centered around global exchange.

Minimal Fees

Today when people talk about cryptocurrency, they are often focused on the *exchange* of cryptocurrency rather than the actual *use* of the currency as a store of value. Let's first shift that mindset to the actual use of cryptocurrency as money used for day-to-day transactions like buying a cup of coffee or even a car.

Businesses have grown accustomed to 3.5% transaction fees on credit cards, which is embraced as a cost of doing business. Cryptocurrency transactions should have the same value of cash transactions for businesses and organizations with the convenience of credit card transactions, but without the fees.

Part of having a transaction that removes a third party also removes the fees involved with a third party. While miners are involved in the blockchain transactions, they are primarily compensated by the network on which they are mining with distributed coins. Because of this, there are often no fees for transacation, and when fees are involved, they are much less than traditional third-party transaction fees because of the minimal effort needed to confirm and secure a transaction on the blockchain.

As there are currently thousands of cryptocurrencies and each one different, fee structures will likely become more consistent and defined in the coming months as norms are formed in cryptocurrency transactions. Regardless, the fees will remain at most a fraction of current transactions and banking fees.

Let's go back to the thought of seeing cryptocurrency as an investment and treating it like stock that is exchanged. In this scenario, fees are necessary just like exchanging stock on the stock exchange or one currency for another. Crypto exchanges though are much more efficient than other exchanges because of the transparency of each currency with the distributed ledger. Since that ledger is accessible on every form of cryptocurrency, it establishes transparent trust in each crypto as well as efficient transactions.

So yes, this means that transactions are cheaper, faster, and more secure via cryptocurrency!

Transparency

Transparency is one of the most debated issues when it comes to cryptocurrencies. While individuals can maintain anonymity when making a transaction through most cryptocurrencies, the amount transacted and agreed upon value exchange of the transaction is transparent. This transparency then exists for the life of the currency as all transactions are then clearly documented on the blockchain and cannot be reversed or removed.

Anonyminity continues to be the most debated aspect of cryptocurrency, as it continues to develop and expand. There is no question that cryptocurrencies have been used for evading taxes, drug trafficking, and other terrible things. Realistically, people have been able to use physical cash to privately do these same things through the years. We are not okay with how this technology has been used in these ways and are glad that measures are being taken to restrict transactions like these in the future.

At the core of the technology is transparency with anonymity, which is a very good thing for security purposes. Regulation has already been established in recent months that has significantly restricted the misuse of crypto for bad, and in the coming months, we expect significant legislation to be adopted that will further restrict illegal exchange and bring great stability to cryptocurrency as a whole.

Transparency is a natural core aspect of cryptocurrency transactions through the blockchain, and as these regulations develop that minimize the opportunity for abuse, cryptocurrencies should thrive in our future economy. The future of this transparent crypto economy with efficient, secure, and transparent exchange is very exciting!

Summary

1. Cryptocurrency transactions offer security by obscuring private data and only making the public key visible to the blockchain.
2. Cryptocurrency transactions are faster.
3. Cryptocurrency transactions are more accessible.
4. Cryptocurrency transactions are cheaper.
5. Cryptocurrency transactions are transparent.

CHAPTER 6

What Others Are Saying about Cryptocurrency

At this point, you might be sold on cryptocurrency. But it's important with every new innovation to be fully aware of all sides of the conversation. The truth is, not everyone loves cryptocurrency.

Doubters have been a reality with every new technology shift throughout history. Very few understood the internet when it was first introduced, and social media was once considered a passing fad. There will always be naysayers and often for good reason.

There are plenty of futuristic ideas that don't catch on. Remember when laser disc players were the next big thing? Or 3D glasses for our televisions? We were also all going to be wearing Google Glass everywhere we went. Some new technologies don't catch on like many predict, and we think it's important to hear what others are saying.

Here are a few comments from naysayers:

> "*Stay away from it. It's a mirage, basically.*" Warren Buffett

> *"We don't really know how this coin is created. You can't have a functional money without a basic transparency. Unless you are addicted to volatile trading for the sake of trading, stay away from the Bitcoin. Thankfully its plunge will be a salutary caution to most folks."* Steve Forbes

> *"There's no fundamental value [with Bitcoin], it's all based on the next guy and the next guy," he says. "Get out if you don't want to lose all of your money because... there's a very good chance it's going to crack. And when it really cracks, you're not going to be able to sell on the way down, there will be no liquidity."* Jordan Belfort, *The Wolf of Wall Street*

These are significant and trusted voices when it comes to money and financial investments. They are worth listening to. Before you panic though, here are a few additional voices also sharing their opinions about Bitcoin and other cryptocurrencies:

> *"Bitcoin is a technological tour de force"* and *"the future of money is digital currency."* Bill Gates

> *"I think the fact that within the Bitcoin universe an algorithm replaces the functions of the government is actually pretty cool. I am a big fan of Bitcoin."* Al Gore

> *"Bitcoin is a remarkable cryptographic achievement and the ability to create something that is not duplicable in the digital*

world has enormous value." Eric Schmidt, Executive Chairman of Google

"Virgin Galactic is a bold entrepreneurial technology. It's driving a revolution. And bitcoin is doing just the same when it comes to inventing a new currency." Richard Branson

There are unlimited opinions on the topic of Bitcoin and cryptocurrency as a whole with new opinions being formed every day. It is important that you form your own opinion and continue to research and understand as this emerging technology and form of currency as it continues to develop.

Our opinion is quite clear that we believe that cryptocurrency is the wave of the future when it comes to currency and transactions. We respect the naysayers and their opinions. There is no doubt that there is much legitimacy to many of the concerns as a great deal of the original use of cryptocurrencies was for drug trafficking and to pay hackers for illegal activity. The reality of the early internet came with the same dark issues, but when we understand both the good and the bad that comes with these new innovations, it is our belief that the negative uses are already being addressed while the positive opportunities are just beginning to be discovered.

As we wrap up this chapter, here's one more comical quote that might best summarize where cryptocurrency is today:

"It's gold for nerds." Stephen Colbert

Summary

1. There is concern about the true value of Bitcoin and other cryptocurrency.
2. Bitcoin and other cryptocurrencies are still highly volatile.
3. There is agreement of the value of the innovation of blockchain technology.
4. Many believe that the future of currency is digital.

CHAPTER 7

Crypto for Good

The creative use of blockchain and cryptocurrencies to advance good and improve lives is something that we are very excited to see emerging in the cryptocurrency space. As entrepreneurs and nonprofit leaders gain a better understanding of how blockchain technology can be applied to accomplish their missions, we're sure to observe the birth of crypto for good.

Most of the publicity around cryptocurrencies has been focused on the volatility of value of crypto currencies with the meteoric rise of the technology and huge valuations of many of the coins along with many of the recent crashes. Speculation about this brave new world of finance are quickly met with questions about the validity of it all and pundits wondering how long Bitcoin and other cryptocurrencies will be around.

Wherever you land in this conversation, one has a difficult time ignoring the fact that cryptocurrencies have shown impressive resilience and viability so far. In a world where powerful players have much to lose with the advent of cryptocurrencies, this new currency continues to exist. For the nonprofit leader, the question now becomes, is this a viable source of revenue? If so, how might the value created in the crypto markets be transferred into mission in the future?

Applying Blockchain to Mission

Following the devastating earthquake of 2010 that caused widespread destruction to an already fragile Haiti, donations for the relief effort began to pour in to organizations helping in the region. An estimated $13 billion was raised to help the people of Haiti in the months that followed the event.

Five years later, compassion gave way to outrage as donors learned that little had changed, and much of the funding had been squandered or lost.[6]

Many of these issues that arose among these nonprofit organizations could have been avoided with the use of blockchain technology and cryptocurrency. The transparency and real-time traceability of blockchain technology promises greater accountability for donors who demand to know how their funds have been used. Imagine tracking the relationship of donations to relief efforts through the supply chain with blockchain-enabled smart contracts. Donors and nonprofit leaders can know

6 https://www.nbcnews.com/news/investigations/what-does-haiti-have-show-13-billion-earthquake-aid-n281661

where money has been sent, how it has been used, and to whom aid has been distributed. This kind of transparency goes a long way to fight against corruption that is so common during relief work in at-risk countries.

Transfer of funds from a central location to field offices become faster and more reliable with the use of cryptocurrency. Instead of couriers carrying and declaring large amounts of cash across borders, a head office can simply make a transfer into the digital wallet of a field office or on-the-ground workers. The transactions are fast, secure, and able to avoid the security risk of currency exchange and transport.

Organizations often raise funds in one location and rely on contractors to accomplish their mission on the ground in another country. Contracted work and payment tracking is simplified when blockchain transparency is applied.

Tracking supply chain, added transparency, and increased security for field workers are just a few ways that blockchain technology will help advance trust between nonprofits and their donors.

Cryptocurrency Donations

Cryptocurrency is still wildly volatile. But this volatility was also the reason why some early adopters have made millions in the space. As agencies like the SEC and IRS begin to craft regulation and tax laws for cryptocurrency, we believe that opportunities to give cryptocurrency as a tax-deductible contribution will continue to rise. This could be a windfall for nonprofits ready to receive these gifts.

In addition to the obvious benefit of receiving a valuable asset to help advance an organization's mission, accepting cryptocurrency donations offers some other advantages that may be appealing to donors. If the opportunity to give crypto for good is promoted properly, nonprofits may even attract new donors to their cause—donors they wouldn't have engaged otherwise.

In 2018, cryptocurrency has a liquidity problem. One can use Bitcoin to purchase some items, but for the most part cryptocurrency holders have trouble exchanging their crypto for goods and services.

When nonprofits begin freely accepting cryptocurrency donations and provide tax-deductible receipts, owners of cryptocurrency have new opportunities for generosity and financial savings. Capital gains taxes apply to cryptocurrency asset growth. Donations to 501(c)3 organizations can offset this tax liability and simultaneously help solve a liquidity problem for cryptocurrency investors.

Nonprofit leaders have long known that some donors prefer to give anonymous gifts to their organizations. Though we think that cryptocurrency donors are more likely to be attracted by the tax benefits, we can't ignore the fact that anonymous donations through cryptocurrency are very attractive to givers who wish to remain unknown.

Ministries and nonprofits regularly see an increase in giving when they choose to offer multiple giving options. I recently learned that churches launching online giving platforms for their congregations can expect an immediate net increase of 10%–20% in giving. Donors like to have options!

If online giving platforms are any indication, nonprofits can expect to see an increase in giving simply by offering cryptocurrency donations as an option to their donor base. Platforms like Engiven (see below) will make it easy for donors to give and simplify the receiving process for nonprofits.

For these reasons, we're beginning to see major nonprofit organizations like Red Cross, United Way, and The Water Project open up their doors to cryptocurrency donations. Future advancements in cryptocurrency giving will help other organizations take advantage of this opportunity too.

Considerations for Cryptocurrency Donations

At present, few nonprofits understand how to accept cryptocurrencies as donations. As a result, the majority of cryptocurrency holders who desire to make charitable contributions must do so in sovereign fiat currencies or navigate a cumbersome process with an organization's accounting team.

This means that for U.S. cryptocurrency holders who desire to make a charitable gift based on gains they may have made in a particular cryptocurrency, the cryptocurrency must first be exchanged into U.S. dollars. Once the cryptocurrency has been liquidated, the donor incurs whatever tax liability is applicable for that particular capital gain. After the tax liability has been satisfied, the donor has less money to give and the nonprofit has less money to receive.

In contrast, had the nonprofit accepted the cryptocurrency directly, the donor could have contributed the entire amount, received the full deduction benefit, and, more importantly, the nonprofit would have received the larger donation.

While 2017 proved to be an important year of growth for the cryptocurrency space, few nonprofits were well positioned in terms of knowledge and technology to benefit from the excess gains and subsequent donations that should have followed thereafter.

So when the founders of Engiven approached us with their vision for their cryptocurrency donation platform, we got very excited. So excited, infact, that we took a personal interest in and became part of the founding team for this cryptocurrency company as well as the formation of a new cryptocurrency that is being created in alignment with the platform.

Because we've been personally involved in the development of a new cryptocurrency and donation platform, we thought it would be interesting to you to open up the hood so you can see what drives the development of a cryptocurrency donation platform and how you can most effectively take advantage of the opportunity today.

Introducing Engiven

At Dunham+Company we are thrilled to work in close partnership with the team at Engiven. Prior to connecting with Engiven, cryptocurrency was something we had begun monitoring closely. We have known the founders of Engiven for many years as they have been technology innovators in the donation space for more than a decade creating one of the first donation platforms centered around SMS/Mobile donations.

When Engiven approached our team at Dunham+Company about the Engiven platform we knew immediately that these were the right guys to lead the way around the emerging opportunities in crypto donations. To see their platform already in action making crypto donations simple for nonprofit organizations and donors is thrilling for our team. It is extremely exciting for us knowing that every nonprofit everywhere can in a matter of minutes begin accepting donations via cryptocurrency and have all of the tools they need to put these donations to work immediately.

Engiven is a software platform that seeks to solve

the problem of accepting cryptocurrency donations for nonprofits. The Engiven platform is the first of its kind… an online application that facilitates peer-to-peer cryptocurrency giving between giver and nonprofit.

It's designed to be a global, membership-based online platform that enables nonprofits to receive cryptocurrencies as donations from individuals. Through the Engiven platform, a nonprofit is provided with all of the online tools needed to accept, store, and exchange any cryptocurrencies from any individual donor.

As crypto-currencies join the mainstream consumer marketplace and government regulations begin to normalize trading and transfer processes, the Engiven team foresees significant opportunities to participate in the facilitation of crypto giving to nonprofits.

Engiven has a goal of giving $1,000,000,000 back to its nonprofit partners. This blockchain supported online platform will be backed by its own cryptocurrency, the ENGV Coin.

ENGV Coins are a key component to the Engiven platform. Each nonprofit member will receive a free allotment of ENGV Coins upon becoming an Engiven Network Member. Additionally, ENGV Coins will be distributed on a scheduled basis to all nonprofit members based upon the coin's utilization. As the ENGV Coins are used (transferred, given, purchased), an allotment of ENGV Coins will be distributed from a reserve pool to every nonprofit Engiven Network Member.

As use of the Engiven platform grows, so does the value and liquidity of the ENGV Coin. Nonprofit members are the beneficiaries with the ability to hold or exchange the ENGV Coin for other cryptocurrencies or fiat currency.

It is our position that cryptocurrencies are here to stay. Every day is met with new reports from organizations like the Securities and Exchange Commission, which signals government organizations are grappling with this new technology and considering how cryptocurrencies might be operated alongside or within our existing financial structures.

The normalization of cryptocurrencies will continue to pave a way for organizations like Engiven to build products and strategies that use crypto for good.

To give you even more insight into the development of a cryptocurrency donation platform like Engiven, we asked the founders of Engiven, Matt Hayes and James Lawrence a series of questions.

Question: *Why did you create Engiven?*

Many cryptocurrencies have been created as an extension of the founders' values or to solve a specific problem. Engiven was created as an extension of our personal values and interests. For many years, Matt and I have endeavored to live and work at the intersection of doing business and doing good. As entrepreneurs, we've been fortunate to experience seasons of massive change in terms of how people think about and use technologies. And we've always believed that generosity should be a lifestyle, not just something you think about once a year or on Sundays. While giving should be personal, it also has to be tangible, something that permeates your worldviews, your purchases, and of course your finances. The products we've created in the past have helped direct consumers' generosity in new and even engaging ways.

Engiven wants to bring generosity into a place that has traditionally been dark and anonymous. Despite some of the media noise, cryptocurrencies can be an important part of our global financial ecosystem. Its anonymous and decentralized nature doesn't mean that it can't be used to benefit humanity. While much of cryptocurrency's past has been shrouded in controversy, doubt, and illicit behavior, we think it's time for cyrpto to grow up a little and become an acceptably used asset for giving, commerce, and overall lifestyle utility. Finally, we decided to build a company in this space because we believe that there's tremendous value and opportunity over the long term. With Engiven, we have taken the road less traveled, so to speak, by participating with the U.S. Securities and Exchange Commission (SEC) to bring to market an SEC approved token. We expect that once the SEC approves our token, ENGV's legitimacy and value will increase. This will enable us to give a large amount of ENGV to the nonprofit community, which we know will benefit a lot of people and a lot of worthy causes.

Question: *Where did the original idea of Engiven come from?*

The concept for Engiven began with a simple idea: to demystify the murky world of crypto and to provide a compelling way for nonprofits to accept crypto as donations. I had been playing around with cryptocurrency for a number of years and also digging into how the Blockchain works. As the cryptocurrency boom of 2017 was in full steam, the environment felt very similar to the late 1990s dotcom rise. I was hearing a lot of the same themes and wild speculations that I heard in the late 90s. It was the Wild West once again. But in every new exploration into uncharted territory, there are great opportunities if you can see past the hype and insanity. Some very important technologies and companies rose out of the dotcom ashes. I began to think about how to use blockchain to the benefit of nonprofits and leverage it to accomplish something good in the world. I had recently sold an online giving software company, and while I had no intention of focusing on giving, I continued to feel strongly about generosity. There was little, if any discussion around crypto and giving, so it became clear there was an opportunity.

Nonprofits are always looking for new ways to engage their audience and grow their donation base. Cryptocurrencies are not much different than other assets that have value and can benefit a nonprofit's mission.

Creating our own token also served to provide a critical piece to the Engiven ecosystem. Our mission is to give away $1 billion worth of ENGV in our first five years. It's pretty exciting to think about the impact that could make.

Question: *Practically, how does Engiven work specifically for nonprofits?*

We've strived to make the process of receiving crypto currency donations really simple. A nonprofit or NGO signs up at engiven.com, and within about three minutes, it creates a widget that can be used to receive cyrpto currency gifts. Our dashboard provides the ability to create a wallet or import existing wallets, where their tokens will be stored. We also provide analytics, videos, and help to demystify the process of giving and receiving crypto currencies. The bottom line: a person who knows almost nothing about crypto currency can quickly get set up and receive donations. Finally, we're working on providing a solution where our nonprofit members can sell and convert their cryptocurrency donations to U.S. dollars. After all, nonprofits operate in fiat currency, which is how they fund their mission.

Question: *Why should nonprofits get on Engiven now?*

We've made the barrier to entry really low. We currently

provide a 90-day free trial and then charge $10 a month or $100 annually for our service. Nonprofits can receive an unlimited amount of cryptocurrency. Also, every nonprofit that signs up will receive free ENGV tokens and also periodic allocations based on the token's overall use in the ecosystem. An organization doesn't need to receive many gifts before this service becomes very valuable.

Question: *What is your dream for the Engiven platform and the future of nonprofits and cryptocurrency?*

Our dream is for Engiven to become a global resource for nonprofits and NGOs, where we provide a tremendous value to the success of their mission. We hope to give away more than $1 billion in the process, which in our minds is the perfect blending of business and philanthropy.

CHAPTER 8

Predictions for the Future

When it comes to cryptocurrency, it seems that there are opinions on all sides of the spectrum. We all have our own opinions about where this is heading! It is interesting today to look back on some of the early predictions about the internet or social media. Twenty years ago, who really would have predicted the rise of Apple or the fall of AOL? Who would have guessed that Facebook, which was created in a college dorm room, would now have over 2 billion active users? In the world of technology, things move fast and the future is often impossible to predict.

While blockchain technology and cryptocurrency isn't completely new, it is still very much being defined with a future that is wide open. It is in no way established, as we are still just on the bleeding edge of this technological development and innovation. Here are some of our predictions for the future of cryptocurrency.

1. There Will Be More

When it comes to the creation and development of cryptocurrencies and blockchain technologies, we are just getting started. There are already thousands of cryptocurrencies, and there likely will be thousands more.

It sounds crazy that at this moment in history anyone anywhere can seemingly just create money. Realistically, anyone could have done this before, whether they created coins or printed paper money. Just because you create a form of currency or money does not mean it is worth anything. The same can be said of most of the cryptocurrencies that are currently being generated.

Let me be clear though. Just because many of the cryptocurrencies are worthless does not mean that all or even most cryptocurrencies are worthless.

Just like we saw in the early days of the internet, there were thousands of websites created on the World Wide Web. Some of these sites took off, like Yahoo and Google, and others fizzled or never even got off the ground.

Just think about the history of the internet and a website like MySpace.com, which was in no way early to the internet. The site quickly became the most popular website on the internet. Then shortly after that spike in popularity, it seemingly faded away after the emergence of Facebook.

In the world of cryptocurrencies, we will likely see thousands of new cryptocurrencies created with most failing, many gaining significant traction, and a handful taking off with mass appeal long term.

It is our opinion that the creation of new cryptocurrencies is just getting started!

2. Regulation Is Coming

Facebook is now more than a decade old. The platform is shaping our culture in more ways than many can even begin to fathom. It is even shaping our political elections, which was made very evident when Mark Zuckerberg, CEO of Facebook, was called before Congress. It was in those sessions that Zuckerberg was asked many questions about data and social media. The proceedings confirmed the government is struggling to understand how to create effective regulations that keep up with the rate of technology innovation.

We have also seen the recent impact of GDPR (General Data Protection Regulation) on many marketers, affecting the way that data can be captured and stored. This is impacting many organizations around the world and the ways that they have grown used to communicating online.

At the writing of this book, there are limited regulations around cryptocurrencies. I think most government officials expected the "fad" of cryptocurrency to fade away by now, and I think many are still just waiting for it to fade away. For those who are paying attention, they are still just beginning to understand the technology and trying to understand how to regulate it.

As shared in Chapter 6, from a taxation standpoint, cryptocurrencies are only taxed when converted to fiat currency—which is why many using cryptocurrencies do not want to convert them, as it decreases the value. In the near future, stronger regulations are likely with a clearer path for how currencies are created and regulated under a greater level of government control.

3. Most Cryptocurrencies Will Fail

We are currently living in the Wild Wild West of Cryptocurrencies, where anyone, anywhere can essentially create a cryptocurrency, release their coins through an Initial Coin Offering, and have a cryptocurrency that anyone can use for exchange of value. As there have been thousands of cryptocurrencies created to date and likely many more to come, it is likely that most will fail. Realistically, only a handful of cryptocurrencies will thrive, while many others survive, and then most will crash.

It is likely that the coming regulation will weed out many of the cryptocurrencies that are not built on a solid structure. These will dissolve and go away. These regulations will also provide stability for many of the cryptocurrencies that have a solid foundation, as well as amplifying those that will thrive for years to come. This weeding out of most cryptocurrencies should actually create greater stability and less volatility for cryptocurrencies as a whole as there will be much less confusion and clutter in the space.

4. Blockchain Technology Will Shape all Sectors

If you can think back to the early days of the internet, it was the World Wide Web and called the Information Super Highway. It still is those things, but also so much more. We use the internet to communicate with each other, to manage or bank accounts, to watch TV, and on and on. The technology innovation of the internet continues to mature and expand, and blockchain technology will do the same.

While blockchain technology has become very popular through its use in the financial sector, the implications of that technology can add value to seemingly every sector. We are already beginning to see many use cases through smart contracts, credentialing, and many other database systems that require third-party proof of a transaction. Even most naysayers of cryptocurrency agree that the development of blockchain technology will be a transformative technology moving into the future.

As more software engineers and developers focus on development around the blockchain, the technology will improve and evolve. As more executives in every sector begin to prioritize innovation built on this new technology, their industry will shift and the technology will expand.

At this point, the question as to whether blockchain technology will infiltrate every sector seems to be less of an *if* question, but rather a *when* question.

What Do You Think?

We want to encourage you to pause at this point in the book and pull your thoughts together about cryptocurrency. What do you think? Where do you think it's going? How should you respond to cryptocurrencies, if at all?